NUTRiBULLET for KIDS

100 Quick and Easy Recipes

By

Celeste Jarabese

Table of Contents

INTRODUCTION

Your child's growing up years is very crucial that is why we must ensure that we are giving them proper nourishment.

Now, you don't have to worry about poor nutrition, with the help of an amazing machine such as the NUTRiBULLET Superfood Extractor you will be able to serve your kids with healthy food.

This book is for mothers with young children who are looking for some healthy ideas to help meet the nutritional requirements of their kids.

The NUTRiBULLET Superfood Extractor provides us with a great solution because it helps break down the food into its simplest form that the body can easily digest. Hence, nutrients are absorbed in a more efficient manner.

Smoothies are very popular because they are very easy to do and there is also a wide variety of ingredients that you can choose from. The use of fresh fruits and vegetables in smoothies can provide your kids with fiber, vitamins, minerals, and antioxidants. While the milk and other dairy products can give them protein and calcium for proper growth and development.

Included in this book are recipes that uses ingredients that can make your kids strong and healthy. Show them how much you care by serving them with these healthy and yummy smoothies.

Get your kids involved in preparing them, trust me it'll be more fun!

Vanilla Cranberry Oat Smoothie With Chia

This delicious smoothie recipe made with cranberries, yogurt, oats, vanilla, and chia is can be served for a quick kiddie breakfast or snack.

Preparation Time: 5 minutes
Total Time: 5 minutes
Yield:1 serving

Ingredients

½ cup cranberries, frozen

½ cup Greek yogurt
2 tablespoon rolled oats
1 teaspoon chia seeds
¼ teaspoon vanilla extract
water to max line

Method

1. Place the cranberries, oats, yogurt, chia seeds, vanilla extract, and water in the tall glass. Process in the NutriBullet for 10-12 seconds or until it becomes smooth.
2. Pour in a serving glass. Garnish with a few cranberries, if desired.
3. Serve and enjoy!

Soy Peach and Banana Shake

This nutrition packed smoothie recipe with soy milk, peach, and banana makes a great grab and go meal whether it is for breakfast or snack.

Preparation Time: 5 minutes
Total Time: 5 minutes
Yield: 1 serving

Ingredients

2/3 cup soy milk
2 peach halves, diced

½ medium banana, sliced
½ cup crushed ice

Method

1. Place the soy milk, peach, banana, and crushed ice in the tall glass. Process in the NutriBullet for 10-12 seconds or until it becomes smooth and creamy.
2. Pour in a chilled tall glass. Garnish with peach or banana slice, if desired.
3. Serve and enjoy!

Triple Citrus Berry and Yogurt Smoothie

This smoothie recipe made with grapefruit, orange, lemon, and raspberries, and Greek yogurt does not only taste good but healthy too!

Preparation Time: 5 minutes
Total Time: 5 minutes
Yield: 1 serving

Ingredients

½ medium grapefruit, cut into segments
½ medium orange, cut into segments
1 Tbsp. lemon juice
¼ cup raspberries, frozen
½ cup Greek yogurt
1 tsp. honey
Water to max line

Method

1. Combine the grapefruit, orange, lemon juice, raspberries, yogurt, and water in the tall glass. Process in the NutriBullet for 10-12 seconds or until it becomes smooth
2. Pour in a serving glass. Garnish with a slice grapefruit or orange, if desired.
3. Serve and enjoy!

Nectarine Ginger Pistachio Smoothie

This ginger-spiced smoothie recipe with nectarines, ginger, and pistachios makes a delicious beverage that you and your kids will surely love.

Preparation Time: 5 minutes
Total Time: 5 minutes
Yield: 1 serving

Ingredients

2 nectarines, sliced
¾ cup skim milk

8 pieces pistachios
½ teaspoon fresh ginger, grated

Method

1. Place nectarines, skim milk, pistachios, and ginger in the tall glass. Process in the NutriBullet for 10-12 seconds or until smooth and creamy.
2. Pour mixture in a serving glass. Garnish with a small slice of nectarine, if desired.
3. Serve and enjoy!

Cranberry Banana and Yogurt Smoothie with Chia

This pink smoothie recipe with cranberries, banana, yogurt, and chia seeds will not only make those little tummies happy but can also make their kidneys healthy.

Preparation Time: 5 minutes
Total Time: 5 minutes
Yield: 1 serving

Ingredients

½ cup frozen cranberries
½ medium banana, sliced
½ cup Greek yogurt
1 tsp. chia seeds
Water to max line

Method

1. Combine the cranberries, banana, yogurt, chia seeds, and water in the tall glass. Process in the NutriBullet for 10-12 seconds or until it becomes smooth.
2. Pour in a serving glass. Garnish with a few cranberries, if desired.
3. Serve and enjoy!

Minty Raspberry Watermelon and Honey Smoothie

This cool and refreshing smoothie recipe with raspberries, watermelon, and honey will help keep your kids stay hydrated especially during hot weather.

Preparation Time: 5 minutes
Total Time: 5 minutes
Yield: 1 serving

Ingredients

½ cup raspberries
½ cup watermelon, cubed
¾ cup skim milk
1 tsp. honey

Method

1. Combine raspberries, watermelon, skim milk, and honey in the tall glass. Process in the NutriBullet for 10-12 seconds or until it becomes smooth.
2. Pour in a serving glass. Garnish with a few raspberries, if desired.
3. Serve and enjoy!

Apple Pear Cucumber and Yogurt Smoothie

This awesome smoothie recipe with apple, pear, cucumber, and yogurt is a great drink if you want something delicious and healthy for snack.

Preparation Time: 5 minutes
Total Time: 5 minutes
Yield: 1 serving

Ingredients

½ medium apple, cored and diced
½ medium pear, cored and diced
½ medium cucumber, diced
½ cup Greek yogurt
¼ cup crushed ice

Method

1. Combine the apple, pear, cucumber, yogurt, and ice cubes in the tall glass. Process in the NutriBullet for 10-12 seconds or until it becomes smooth.
2. Pour in a serving glass. Garnish with a slice of apple or pear, if desired.
3. Serve and enjoy!

Raspberry Banana and Coconut Smoothie with Mint

This scrumptious smoothie recipe with raspberries, banana, coconut milk, and coconut water makes great refreshment any time of the day.

Preparation Time: 5 minutes
Total Time: 5 minutes
Yield: 1 serving

Ingredients

½ cup raspberries, frozen
½ medium bananas cut into small pieces
2 tablespoons coconut milk
½ cup coconut water
1 mint sprig

Method

1. Combine the raspberries, banana, coconut milk, coconut water, and mint in the tall glass. Process in the NutriBullet for 10-12 seconds or until it becomes smooth.
2. Pour in a serving glass. Garnish with few raspberries and mint sprig, if desired.
3. Serve and enjoy!

Fiber Rich Raspberry Almond Smoothie

This smoothie recipe with raspberries, almond milk, and wheat germ makes a healthy breakfast or snack in a glass!

Preparation Time: 5 minutes
Total Time: 5 minutes
Yield: 1 serving

Ingredients

3/4 cup raspberries
2/3 cup almond milk, unsweetened
2 tablespoons wheat germ
1 teaspoon honey
1-2 ice cubes

Method

1. Place raspberries, almond milk, and wheat germ, honey, and ice in the tall glass. Process in the NutriBullet for 10-12 seconds or until combined well.
2. Pour in a serving glass with ice. Garnish with few raspberries, if desired.
3. Serve and enjoy!

Strawberry Banana and Lettuce Smoothie

This is a wonderful pink smoothie recipe made with strawberries, banana, iceberg lettuce and almond milk. If you want to try something new that will give your kids loads of nutrients this is the recipe for you.

Preparation Time: 5 minutes
Total Time: 5 minutes
Yield: 1 serving

Ingredients

½ cup strawberry
1 small banana, sliced
2 pcs.Iceberg lettuce leaves, shredded
2/3 cup almond milk, unsweetened
2 ice cubes

Method

1. In the tall glass, place the strawberries, banana, lettuce, almond milk, and ice cubes. Process in the NutriBullet for 10-12 seconds or until smooth.
2. Transfer mixture in a serving glass with ice. Garnish with a small strawberry, if desired.
3. Serve and enjoy!

Soya Banana Choco and Oat Smoothie

This is a very delicious and rich smoothie recipe made with soya, banana, cocoa, and oats. Your kids will surely enjoy it!

Preparation Time: 5 minutes
Total Time: 5 minutes
Yield: 1 serving

Ingredients

¾ cup soya milk
1 small banana, sliced
1 Tbsp. cocoa powder
2 Tbsp. rolled oats

Method

1. In the tall glass, place the soya milk, banana, cocoa powder, and oats. Process in the NutriBullet for 10-12 seconds or until smooth.
2. Pour mixture in a serving glass. Sprinkle with some cocoa powder, if desired.
3. Serve and enjoy!

Coconut Orange and Honey Slush

This tasty tropical drink with coconut water, orange, and honey will provide your kids with good amounts of potassium and vitamin C that promotes wellness.

Preparation Time: 5 minutes
Total Time: 5 minutes
Yield: 1 serving

Ingredients

1 medium orange, cut into segments
1 teaspoon honey
½ cup crushed ice
Coconut water to max line

Method

1. Combine the orange, honey, crushed ice, and coconut water in the tall glass. Process in the NutriBullet for 10-12 seconds or until smooth.
2. Transfer mixture in a serving glass. Garnish with a slice of orange, if desired.
3. Serve and enjoy!

Strawberry Hemp and Yogurt Smoothie

This smoothie recipe with strawberries, hemp seeds, and yogurt makes a great breakfast, dessert or afternoon pick-me-up because it is equipped with many vital nutrients.

Preparation Time: 5 minutes
Total Time: 5 minutes
Yield: 1 serving

Ingredients

¾ cup strawberries, hulled, halved
1 teaspoon hemp seeds
½ cup vanilla yogurt
¼ cup whole milk

Method

1. Place the strawberries, hemp seeds, vanilla yogurt, and milk in the tall glass. Process in the NutriBullet for 10-12 seconds or until combined well.
2. Pour in a chilled serving glass. Garnish with strawberry, if desired.
3. Serve and enjoy!

Honeydew Apple and Yogurt Smoothie

This mouthwatering yogurt smoothie recipe is made with honeydew melon and apple. It is good for your kids because of the many health benefits it can provide.

Preparation Time: 5 minutes
Total Time: 5 minutes
Yield: 1 serving

Ingredients

½ cup honeydew melon, cubed
1 medium green apple, peeled, cored, and diced
½ cup Greek yogurt, plain
½ cup crushed ice

Method

1. Combine the honeydew melon, apple, yogurt, and crushed ice in the tall glass. Process in the NutriBullet for 10-12 seconds or until it becomes smooth.
2. Pour mixture in a serving glass. Garnish with a small slice of apple or melon, if desired.
3. Serve and enjoy!

Strawberry Almond Milkshake with Walnuts

This wonderful smoothie made with strawberries, almond milk, and walnuts is rich in fiber, vitamin C for healthy body.

Preparation Time: 5 minutes
Total Time: 5 minutes
Yield: 1 serving

Ingredients

¾ cup strawberries
½ cup almond milk
4 pcs. Walnuts
2 ice cubes

Method

1. Place strawberries, almond milk, walnuts and ice cubes in the tall glass. Process in the NutriBullet for 10-12 seconds or until smooth and creamy.
2. Pour mixture in a chilled glass. Garnish with strawberry, if desired.
3. Serve and enjoy!

Minty Strawberry Shake with Sunflower Seeds

This delicious smoothie recipe with strawberries, mint and sunflower seeds contain healthy carbs and fats plus antioxidants which can help your kids stay away from different kind of illnesses.

Preparation Time: 5 minutes
Total Time: 5 minutes
Yield: 1 serving

Ingredients

¾ cup strawberries, halved
½ cup whole milk
1 Tbsp. sunflower seeds
1 mint sprig
1-2 ice cubes

Method

1. Combine strawberries, whole milk, sunflower seeds, mint, and ice cubes in the tall glass. Place and process in the NutriBullet for 10-12 seconds or until becomes smooth.
2. Pour in a serving glass. Garnish with strawberry and mint sprig, if desired.
3. Serve and enjoy!

Choco Banana Oatmeal Smoothie

Oatmeal is incredibly healthy and filling, but let's faces it; your kids don't really like it, do they?! This is an excellent trick to make them have oatmeal – a smoothie that tastes like dessert but has plenty of health benefits.

Preparation Time: 5 minutes
Total Time: 5 minutes
Yield: 1 serving

Ingredients

2 tablespoons raw cocoa powder + 2 tablespoons hot water
¼ cup oatmeal, cooked
2 tablespoons raw almonds
1 small banana
½ cup whole milk

Method

1. Combine cocoa powder, oatmeal, almonds, banana, and milk in the tall glass. Process in the NutriBullet for 10-12 seconds or until mixture becomes smooth.
2. Transfer mixture in a serving glass.
3. Serve and enjoy!

Green Oreo Smoothie

Everyone loves Oreo, especially the kids. Together with a vegetable, it will not be only delicious, but also nutritious.

Preparation Time: 5 minutes
Total Time: 5 minutes
Yield: 1 serving

Ingredients

½ cup crushed Oreo cookies
½ cup baby spinach
¾ cup almond milk, unsweetened
¼ teaspoon vanilla extract
1-2 ice cubes

Method

1. Combine Oreo cookies, spinach, almond milk, vanilla extract and ice in the tall glass. Process in the NutriBullet for 10-12 seconds or until mixture becomes smooth.
2. Transfer mixture in a serving glass.
3. Serve and enjoy!

Papaya Banana Soy and Walnut Smoothie

This luscious smoothie recipe with papaya, banana, soy milk, and walnuts is loaded with essential nutrients that will ensure your kids will get enough supply of energy.

Preparation Time: 5 minutes
Total Time: 5 minutes
Yield: 1 serving

Ingredients

¾ cup papaya, cubed
1small banana, sliced
6 pieces walnut halves
½ cup soy milk

Method

1. Place papaya, banana, walnuts, and soy milk into the tall glass. Process in the NutriBullet for 10-12 seconds or until becomes smooth.
2. Pour in a chilled serving glass. Garnish with a slice of papaya, if desired.
3. Serve and enjoy!

Peanut Butter Chocolate and Almond Smoothie

Love this nutty chocolaty smoothie that will definitely satisfy your kid's sweet cravings.

Preparation Time: 5 minutes
Total Time: 5 minutes
Yield: 1 serving

Ingredients

2 tablespoons peanut butter
3 tablespoons dark chocolate, melted
¾ cup almond milk
2 ice cubes

Method

1. Combine peanut butter, dark chocolate, protein powder, almond milk, and ice cubes in the tall glass. Process in the NutriBullet for 10-12 seconds or until mixture becomes smooth.
2. Transfer mixture in a serving glass.
3. Serve and enjoy!

Banana Peanut Butter Chocolate Smoothie

Who doesn't love peanut butter? Kids and grown-ups alike will love this smoothie, not only its thick consistency, but also its rich taste and incredible aroma.

Preparation Time: 5 minutes
Total Time: 5 minutes
Yield: 1 serving

Ingredients

1 small banana, sliced
2 tablespoon smooth peanut butter
2 tablespoon dark chocolate, melted
½ cup whole milk
2 ice cubes

Method

1. Combine banana, peanut butter, dark chocolate, skim milk, chia seeds and raw almonds in the tall glass. Process in the NutriBullet for 10-12 seconds or until mixture becomes smooth.
2. Transfer mixture in a serving glass.
3. Serve and enjoy!

Banana Peanut Butter Oatmeal Smoothie

This peanut butter oatmeal smoothie is not only delicious, but also nutritious. It may be a simple recipe but it stands out through its delicate and rich taste.

Preparation Time: 5 minutes
Total Time: 5 minutes
Yield: 1 serving

Ingredients

1 small banana, sliced
2 tablespoon smooth peanut butter
¼ cup oatmeal, cooked
¾ cups whole milk
½ teaspoon vanilla extract

Method

1. Combine banana, peanut butter, oatmeal, whole milk and vanilla extract in the tall glass. Process in the NutriBullet for 10-12 seconds or until mixture becomes smooth.
2. Transfer mixture in a serving glass.
3. Serve and enjoy!

Raspberry Banana and Coconut Smoothie

This healthy and tasty smoothie recipe is loaded with fiber, vitamins, and minerals from the raspberries, banana, milk, and coconut water. Coconut water hydrates the body and also rich in minerals that supports good health.

Preparation Time: 5 minutes
Total Time: 5 minutes
Yield: 1 serving

Ingredients

¾ cup raspberries, frozen
1 medium banana, sliced
½ cup whole milk
Coconut water to max line

Method

1. Combine raspberries, banana, milk, and coconut water in the tall glass. Process in the NutriBullet for 10-12 seconds or until becomes smooth.
2. Pour in a serving glass. Garnish with a few raspberries and banana slices, if desired.
3. Serve and enjoy!

Spinach Banana and Yogurt Smoothie

This recipe is a winner when it comes to masking the taste of spinach. There is a huge chance that your kids will love it and it is definitely worth a try if they're not fond of eating veggies.

Preparation Time: 5 minutes
Total Time: 5 minutes
Yield: 1 serving

Ingredients

½ cup fresh spinach
1 medium banana
½ cup vanilla yogurt
¼ cup whole milk
2 ice cubes

Method

1. Combine spinach, banana, and yogurt, milk, and ice cubes in the tall glass. Process in the NutriBullet for 10-12 seconds or until mixture becomes smooth.
2. Transfer mixture in a serving glass.
3. Serve and enjoy!

Strawberry and Vanilla Ice Cream Shake

Is there anything better than a glass of chilled shake during summer? Definitely not! This shake is better than simple ice cream because it's not only sweet and refreshing but also healthy and nutritious.

Preparation Time: 5 minutes
Total Time: 5 minutes
Yield: 1 serving

Ingredients

½ cup fresh strawberries
½ cup low fat vanilla ice cream
¼ cup yogurt
¼ cup whole milk

Method

1. Combine strawberries, ice cream, yogurt, and milk in the tall glass. Process in the NutriBullet for 10-12 seconds or until mixture becomes smooth.
2. Transfer mixture in a serving glass.
3. Serve and enjoy!

Strawberry and Yogurt Super Healthy Smoothie

Both strawberries and yogurt make a nice addition to your daily diet, but if you combine them you get a super healthy and super delicious drink that can be enjoyed by the entire family.

Preparation Time: 5 minutes
Total Time: 5 minutes
Yield: 1 serving

Ingredients

½ cup fresh strawberries
½ cup plain yogurt
¼ cup whole milk
1 teaspoon chia seeds
1 teaspoon honey

Method

1. Combine strawberries, yogurt, almond milk, chia seeds and honey in the tall glass. Process in the NutriBullet for 10-12 seconds or until mixture becomes smooth.
2. Transfer mixture in a serving glass.
3. Serve and enjoy!

Tofu Blueberry Honey Smoothie

This smoothie recipe with tofu, blueberries, soy milk, and honey makes a great afternoon snack or quick breakfast. It is loaded with important nutrients for healthier kids!

Preparation Time: 5 minutes
Total Time: 5 minutes
Yield: 1 serving

Ingredients

½ cup blueberries
½ cup soft tofu
½ cup soy milk
1 teaspoon honey

Method

1. Place blueberries, tofu, soy milk, and honey into the tall glass. Process in the NutriBullet for 10-12 seconds or until becomes smooth.
2. Pour in a chilled serving glass. Garnish with a few blueberries, if desired.
3. Serve and enjoy!

Tutti-frutti Super Healthy Smoothie

How about a drink that combines the fragrance of strawberries with the taste of orange and banana? It's an amazing drink that doesn't only have an incredible taste, but it is also loaded with nutrients to boost your kid's health.

Preparation Time: 5 minutes
Total Time: 5 minutes
Yield: 1 serving

Ingredients

½ cup fresh strawberries
½ medium orange, cut into segments
½ medium banana, sliced
½ cup whole milk

Method

1. Combine strawberries, orange, banana, and milk in the tall glass. Process in the NutriBullet for 10-12 seconds or until mixture becomes smooth.
2. Transfer mixture in a serving glass.
3. Serve and enjoy!

Very Berry Oatmeal Smoothie

Fragrant and rich, this smoothie will impress everyone, from kids to grown-ups. But its advantage is not on the taste, but the nutritional profile – it is loaded with antioxidants, fibers and vitamins.

Preparation Time: 5 minutes
Total Time: 5 minutes
Yield: 1 serving

Ingredients

½ cup wild berries
2 tablespoons rolled oats
½ cup whole milk
¼ cup vanilla yogurt
1 teaspoon honey

Method

1. Combine wild berries, rolled oats, milk, yogurt, and honey in the tall glass. Process in the NutriBullet for 10-12 seconds or until mixture becomes smooth.
2. Transfer mixture in a serving glass.
3. Serve and enjoy!

Mixed Berry Banana Almond Smoothie

This smoothie has such an intense flavor that you kids will enjoy. Needless to say that is also high in antioxidants and a great energy booster!

Preparation Time: 5 minutes
Total Time: 5 minutes
Yield: 1 serving

Ingredients

½ cup frozen mixed berries
1 small banana
½ cup whole milk
6 pcs. Dry roasted almonds

Method

1. Combine mixed berries, banana, milk, and almonds in the tall glass. Process in the NutriBullet for 10-12 seconds or until mixture becomes smooth.
2. Transfer mixture in a serving glass.
3. Serve and enjoy!

Watermelon Apple and Yogurt Smoothie

This refreshing yogurt smoothie recipe made with watermelon, apple, wheat germ, and yogurt is packed with amazing flavors and nutrients that are good for the body.

Preparation Time: 5 minutes
Total Time: 5 minutes
Yield: 1 serving

Ingredients

1 cup seedless watermelon, cubed
½ medium apple, peeled, cored, and diced
½ cup Greek yogurt, plain
1 tablespoon wheat germ

Method

1. Combine the watermelon, apple, yogurt, wheat germ, and water in the tall glass. Process in the NutriBullet for 10-12 seconds or until it becomes smooth.
2. Pour mixture in a serving glass. Garnish with a small slice of watermelon, if desired.
3. Serve and enjoy!

Banana Yogurt Milkshake

Frozen yogurt is healthier than ice cream and still yields a delicious smoothie.

Preparation Time: 5minutes
Total Time: 5 minutes
Yield: 1 serving

Ingredients

1 medium ripe banana
½ cup frozen yogurt

½ cup whole milk
¼ teaspoon vanilla extract

Method

1. Combine all the ingredients in your Nutribullet and pulse 10-20 seconds or until smooth.
2. Pour in glasses and serve immediately.

Blueberry Kiwi and Soy Yogurt Smoothie

This smoothie recipe with blueberries, kiwi, soy yogurt, and wheat germ makes a refreshing morning or afternoon snack. It is loaded with essential nutrients for stronger immunity against illness.

Preparation Time: 5minutes
Total Time: 5 minutes
Yield: 1 serving

Ingredients

½ cup blueberries
½ medium kiwi fruit, diced
½ cup soy yogurt, plain or vanilla
1 tablespoon wheat germ
Water to max line

Method

1. Place blueberries, kiwi, soy yogurt, and wheat germ, and water into the tall glass. Process in the NutriBullet for 10-12 seconds or until becomes smooth.
2. Pour in a chilled serving glass. Garnish with a few blueberries or a slice of kiwi, if desired.
3. Serve and enjoy!

Carrot and Mango Smoothie

Both carrot and mango have a high content of beta-carotene so the final drink is not only fragrant and delicious, but also highly nutritious.

Preparation Time: 5minutes
Total Time: 5 minutes
Yield: 1 serving

Ingredients

1 cup fresh carrot juice

1 medium ripe mango, diced
4 ice cubes

Method

1. Combine all the ingredients in your Nutribullet and pulse until smooth.
2. Pour the drink in glasses of your choice and serve immediately.

Choco Banana and Apple Smoothie

This delicious smoothie recipe with cocoa, banana, and apple is great for an afternoon snack or dessert.

Preparation Time: 5minutes
Total Time: 5 minutes
Yield: 1 serving

Ingredients

1 tablespoon cocoa powder + 2 tablespoons hot water
½ medium bananas cut into small pieces
½ medium apple, cored and diced
¾ cup whole milk
2 ice cubes

Method

1. Place cocoa powder, banana, apple, milk and ice cubes in the tall glass. Place and process in the NutriBullet for 10-12 seconds or until smooth.
2. Pour in a serving glass.
3. Serve and enjoy!

Super Healthy Mango Banana and Oat Smoothie

The tropical flavors of this smoothie are a real delight even for the pickiest eaters out there.

Preparation Time: 5 minutes
Total Time: 5 minutes
Yield: 1 serving

Ingredients

½ medium ripe mango, diced
½ medium ripe banana, sliced
2 tablespoon rolled oats
2/3 cup whole milk
2 ice cubes

Method

1. Combine mango, banana, rolled oats, milk, and ice cubes in the tall glass. Process in the NutriBullet for 10-12 seconds or until mixture becomes smooth.
2. Transfer mixture in a serving glass.
3. Serve and enjoy!

Orange and Cranberry Milkshake

This refreshing milkshake is your best friend during summer. Take advantage of its nourishing, refreshing and amazing taste at any time of the day and serve it chilled for an intensive cooling effect.

Preparation Time: 5 minutes
Total Time: 5 minutes
Yield: 1 serving

Ingredients

½ medium orange, cut into segments
¼ cup fresh cranberries
½ cup whole milk
¼ cup plain yogurt
1 teaspoon honey

Method

1. Combine orange, cranberries, milk, yogurt, and honey in the tall glass. Process in the NutriBullet for 10-12 seconds or until mixture becomes smooth.
2. Transfer mixture in a serving glass.
3. Serve and enjoy!

Yummy Orange and Strawberry Smoothie

You will never know how delicious this drink is before you try it. The strawberries are fragrant and the orange is refreshing, but they are combined into a drink that is nourishing, refreshing and can cool you down during those hot summer days.

Preparation Time: 5 minutes
Total Time: 5 minutes
Yield: 1 serving

Ingredients

½ cup fresh strawberries, halved
½ medium orange, cut into segments
½ cup whole milk
¼ cup plain yogurt

Method

1. Combine strawberries, orange, milk, yogurt in the tall glass. Process in the NutriBullet for 10-12 seconds or until mixture becomes smooth.
2. Transfer mixture in a serving glass.
3. Serve and enjoy!

Delightful Orange Banana Yogurt Shake

This shake is all about the nutrients, refreshing taste and the fragrance of combined fruits and needless to say that it tastes heavenly!

Preparation Time: 5 minutes
Total Time: 5 minutes
Yield: 1 serving

Ingredients

½ Mandarin orange segments
1 small banana, sliced
½ cup Greek yogurt
¼ cup whole milk

Method

1. Combine orange, banana, yogurt, and milk the tall glass. Process in the NutriBullet for 10-12 seconds or until mixture becomes smooth.
2. Transfer mixture in a serving glass.
3. Serve and enjoy!

Pineapple Orange Yogurt Smoothie

Having an intense pineapple and orange flavor, this smoothie is a real healthy delight that will bring joy to your taste buds for sure.

Preparation Time: 5 minutes
Total Time: 5 minutes
Yield: 1 serving

Ingredients

½ cup pineapple chunks
½ medium orange, cut into segments
½ cup Greek yogurt
2 ice cubes

Method

1. Combine pineapple chunks, orange segments, yogurt, and ice cubes in the tall glass. Process in the NutriBullet for 10-12 seconds or until mixture becomes smooth.
2. Transfer mixture in a serving glass.
3. Serve and enjoy!

Mango and Kiwi Oatmeal Smoothie

The amazing flavors of this healthy smoothie are a real delight even for the pickiest eaters.

Preparation Time: 5 minutes
Total Time: 5 minutes
Yield: 1 serving

Ingredients

½ medium ripe mango, diced
½ medium kiwi fruit, diced
¼ cup oatmeal, cooked
2/3 cup whole milk

Method

1. Combine the mango, kiwi, oatmeal, and milk in the tall glass. Process in the NutriBullet for 10-12 seconds or until mixture becomes smooth.
2. Transfer mixture in a serving glass.
3. Serve and enjoy!

Mango and Coconut Chilled Smoothie

Simple recipes are often the best and this one makes no exception. The list of ingredients is short and the time spent preparing this drink is just as short, but the final drink is incredibly tasty, healthy and refreshing!

Preparation Time: 5 minutes
Total Time: 5 minutes

Yield: 1 serving

Ingredients

¾ cup ripe mango
½ cup coconut water
2 Tbsp. coconut milk
1 teaspoon agave nectar
2 ice cubes

Method

1. Combine mango, coconut water,coconut milk, agave syrup, and ice cubes in the tall glass. Process in the NutriBullet for 10-12 seconds or until mixture becomes smooth.
2. Transfer mixture in a serving glass.
3. Serve and enjoy!

Mandarin Vanilla Yogurt and Chia Smoothie

This is a great smoothie recipe made with Mandarin orange, yogurt, milk, and chia seeds.

Preparation Time: 5 minutes
Total Time: 5 minutes
Yield:1 serving

Ingredients

1 medium Mandarin orange segments
½ cup plain yogurt
¼ cup whole milk
1 tsp. chia seeds
½ cup crushed ice

Method

1. Combine Mandarin orange segments, yogurt, milk, and chia seeds, and ice in the tall glass. Process in the NutriBullet for 10-12 seconds or until mixture becomes smooth.
2. Transfer mixture in a serving glass.
3. Serve and enjoy!

Avocado Banana and Chia Shake

A cool and refreshing drink made with avocado, banana, and chia seeds. It is great for a hot summer day.

Preparation Time: 5 minutes
Total Time: 5 minutes
Yield:1 serving

Ingredients

¼ ripe avocado
1 medium banana, sliced
¾ cup whole milk
1 teaspoon chia seeds
¼ crushed ice

Method

1. Combine avocado, banana, milk, chia seeds, and ice in the tall glass. Process in the NutriBullet for 10-12 seconds or until mixture becomes smooth.
2. Transfer mixture in serving glass.
3. Serve and enjoy!

Banana and Strawberry Oatmeal Milkshake

Unlike other smoothies, this milkshake is richer, thicker and has an intense fruity taste that your kids will surely love.

Preparation Time: 5 minutes
Total Time: 5 minutes
Yield:1 serving

Ingredients

1 small banana, sliced
¼ cup fresh strawberries
2 tablespoon rolled oats
1 scoop low fat vanilla ice cream
½ cup whole milk

Method

1. Combine banana, strawberries, rolled oats, vanilla ice cream, andmilk in the tall glass. Process in the NutriBullet for 10-12 seconds or until mixture becomes smooth.
2. Transfer mixture in a serving glass.
3. Serve and enjoy!

Almond Banana Milkshake

This shake is creamy and thick, what your kids need to boost their energy during those hot summer days.

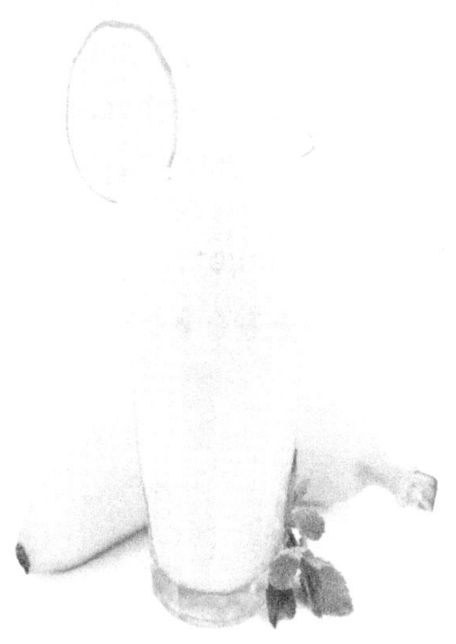

Preparation Time: 5 minutes
Total Time: 5 minutes
Yield:1 serving

Ingredients

1 small banana, peeled and cut

1 scoop low fat vanilla ice cream
¾ cup almond milk
2 tsp. lime juice

Method

1. Combine banana, vanilla ice cream, almond milk, and lime juice in the tall glass. Process in the NutriBullet for 10-12 seconds or until mixture becomes smooth.
2. Transfer mixture in a serving glass.
3. Serve and enjoy!

Strawberry and Chocolate Duo Smoothie

This shake has a beautiful color contrast, but also an amazing taste and it combines two flavors: strawberry and chocolate. Just be careful because it gets addictive!

Preparation Time: 5 minutes
Total Time: 5 minutes
Yield:1 serving

Ingredients

Strawberry layer:
½ cup fresh strawberries
½ cup almond milk
¼ cup plain yogurt

Chocolate layer:
½ cup low fat chocolate ice cream
2 tablespoons chocolate sauce
¼ cup almond milk

Method

1. To make the first layer, combine the strawberries with almond milk andyogurt in your Nutribullet and pulse until smooth and well blended.
2. Pour the first layer in glasses and set aside.
3. To make the second layer, mix all the ingredients in your Nutribullet and process until smooth.
4. Gently pour the chocolate smoothie over the strawberry one. Garnish with chocolate shavings, if desired.
5. Serve right away.

Oatmeal Milkshake

Your kid's morning meal couldn't be better than with this smoothie! It's refreshing and healthy, perfect for a great start of the day!

Preparation Time: 5 minutes
Total Time: 5 minutes
Yield:1 serving

Ingredients

1 small frozen banana, sliced
¼ cup oatmeal, cooked
2/3 cup almond milk
1 tsp. hemp seeds

Method

1. Combine banana, oatmeal, almond milk, and hemp seeds in the tall glass. Process in the NutriBullet for 10-12 seconds or until mixture becomes smooth.
2. Transfer mixture in a serving glass. Garnish with chocolate sauce, if desired.
3. Serve and enjoy!

Banana Nutella Smoothie

Your kids will love this creamy and thick smoothie with Nutella! With banana and milk, this is all you need to give them for a healthy and filling drink.

Preparation Time: 5 minutes
Total Time: 5 minutes
Yield:1 serving

Ingredients

1 small banana, sliced
1 tablespoon Nutella
¾ cup whole milk
¼ cup crushed ice

Method

1. Combine banana, Nutella, skim milk and yogurt in the tall glass. Process in the NutriBullet for 10-12 seconds or until mixture becomes smooth.
2. Transfer mixture in a serving glass.
3. Serve and enjoy!

Blueberry Banana and Ricotta Smoothie

This delectable smoothie recipe with blueberries, banana, ricotta, and skim milk is loaded with nutrients such as healthy carbohydrates, protein, and fiber. A complete meal in minutes!

Preparation Time: 5 minutes
Total Time: 5 minutes
Yield:1 serving

Ingredients

½ cup frozen blueberries
½ medium banana, cut into small pieces
½ cup whole milk
¼ cup ricotta cheese

Method

1. Combine blueberries, banana, milk, and ricotta cheese, in the tall glass. Place and process in the NutriBullet for 10-12 seconds or until becomes smooth.
2. Pour in a serving glass. Garnish with a few blueberries, if desired.
3. Serve and enjoy!

Chilled Delicious Breakfast Smoothie

Breakfast during summer has to be nutritious and yet light and refreshing and this recipe is your best option because it has everything you need for a great day ahead.

Preparation Time: 5 minutes
Total Time: 5 minutes

Yield:1 serving

Ingredients

½ cup frozen mixed berries
1 small banana, peeled and cubed
1 tablespoon rolled oats
2/3 cup almond milk
1 teaspoon chia seeds

Method

1. Combine the berries, banana, rolled oats, almond milk, and chia seeds in the tall glass. Process in the NutriBullet for 10-12 seconds or until mixture becomes smooth.
2. Transfer mixture in a serving glass. Garnish with a slice of banana or few berries, if desired.
3. Serve and enjoy!

Chilled Pomegranate Smoothie

Pomegranate has a high content of vitamin C which is amazing during those hot summer days because it can keep your kids hydrated and gives them the needed energy to go on with their daily tasks.

Preparation Time: 5 minutes
Total Time: 5 minutes
Yield:1 serving

Ingredients

½ cup fresh pomegranate seeds
1 small banana, peeled and cut
½ cup vanilla yogurt
¼ cup crushed ice

Method

1. Combine pomegranate seeds, banana, yogurt, and crushed ice in the tall glass. Process in the NutriBullet for 10-12 seconds or until mixture becomes smooth.
2. Transfer mixture in a serving glass.
3. Serve and enjoy!

Chocolate Orange and Almond Smoothie

Orange with chocolate and almond will always impress even the pickiest eaters. They balance each other so the final drink is smooth, tangy, sweet, and absolutely delicious, and at the same time healthy.

Preparation Time: 5 minutes
Total Time: 5 minutes
Yield:1 serving

Ingredients

½ medium orange, cut into segments
1 tablespoon cocoa powder + 1 tablespoon hot water
1 tablespoon chocolate syrup
¾ cup almond milk

Method

1. Combine orange, cocoa powder, chocolate syrup,and almond milk in the tall glass. Process in the NutriBullet for 10-12 seconds or until mixture becomes smooth.
2. Transfer mixture in a serving glass.
3. Serve and enjoy!

Chocolate and Raspberry Smoothie

Chocolate and raspberry is a combination that never fails to deliver an incredible taste, a rich and smooth consistency and healthy. You will love this drink for sure!

Preparation Time: 5 minutes
Total Time: 5 minutes
Yield:1 serving

Ingredients

½ cup fresh raspberries
2/3 cup whole milk
1 tablespoon chocolate syrup
¼ teaspoon vanilla extract
2 ice cubes

Method

1. Combine raspberries, milk, chocolate syrup, vanilla extract, and ice in the tall glass. Process in the NutriBullet for 10-12 seconds or until mixture becomes smooth.
2. Transfer mixture in a serving glass.
3. Serve and enjoy!

Blueberry Almond and Flax Smoothie

Blueberries are definitely underestimated. In fact, they are the berries with one of the highest content of vitamins and antioxidants and introducing them into your child's diet is definitely a smart move.

Preparation Time: 5 minutes
Total Time: 5 minutes
Yield:1 serving

Ingredients

½ cup fresh or frozen blueberries
¾ cup almond milk
1 teaspoon flaxseeds
1 teaspoon honey
¼ cup crushed ice

Method

1. Combine blueberries, almond milk, flaxseeds, honey, and crushed ice in the tall glass. Process in the NutriBullet for 10-12 seconds or until mixture becomes smooth.
2. Transfer mixture in a serving glass.
3. Serve and enjoy!

Chilled Soy Chocolate and Banana Smoothie

Chocolate can be refreshing! This smoothie is the best proof from every point of view. It's creamy, rich and nutritious, amazingly delicious.

Preparation Time: 5 minutes
Total Time: 5 minutes
Yield:1 serving

Ingredients

2/3 cup soy milk, chocolate flavor
1 small banana
1 Tbsp. chocolate syrup
½ cup crushed ice

Method

1. Combine soy milk, banana, chocolate syrup, and crushed ice in the tall glass. Process in the NutriBullet for 10-12 seconds or until mixture becomes smooth.
2. Transfer mixture in a serving glass.
3. Serve and enjoy!

Creamy Peach and Cottage Smoothie

So creamy and so delicious! This smoothie combines the rich taste of peach and cottage cheese, but it is also as healthy as a smoothie can be, having a good amount of protein, fiber and antioxidants.

Preparation Time: 5 minutes
Total Time: 5 minutes
Yield:1 serving

Ingredients
2 peach halves
½ cup cottage cheese
½ cup whole milk
¼ teaspoon vanilla extract
1 teaspoon honey

Method
1. Combine peach halves, cottage cheese, milk, vanilla, and honey in the tall glass. Process in the NutriBullet for 10-12 seconds or until mixture becomes smooth.
2. Transfer mixture in a serving glass.
3. Serve and enjoy!

Citrus Raisin and Oat Smoothie

Raisins are a great source of nutrients but they need something tangy to balance their sweet taste. Citrus fruits are exactly what this smoothie needs to turn into a fresh and delicious drink that will brighten your kids' morning.

Preparation Time: 5 minutes
Total Time: 5 minutes
Yield:1 serving

Ingredients

½ medium orange, cut into segments
¼ cup raisins
2 Tbsp. rolled oats
¼ cup plain yogurt
½ cup whole milk

Method

1. Combine the orange, raisins, oats, yogurt, and milk in the tall glass. Process in the NutriBullet for 10-12 seconds or until mixture becomes smooth.
2. Transfer mixture in a serving glass.
3. Serve and enjoy!

Citrus Banana Almond Smoothie

Rich and yet refreshing, this smoothie is best served in the morning when your kids need as much energy as possible to make sure they start the day on a high note.

Preparation Time: 5 minutes
Total Time: 5 minutes
Yield:1 serving

Ingredients

½ cup Mandarin orange segments
½ medium banana
¼ cup plain yogurt
½ cup almond milk
2 tsp. lemon juice
1 teaspoon honey

Method

1. Combine orange segments, banana, yogurt, almond milk, lemon juice, and honey in the tall glass. Process in the NutriBullet for 10-12 seconds or until mixture becomes smooth.
2. Transfer mixture in a serving glass.
3. Serve and enjoy!

Double Chocolate Banana Smoothie

Kids love chocolates, treat them with this chocolaty smoothie that will surely satisfy your kid's sweet cravings.

Preparation Time: 5 minutes
Total Time: 5 minutes
Yield:1 serving

Ingredients

¾ cup nonfat chocolate milk
1 tablespoon dark chocolate, melted
1 small banana, sliced
¼ teaspoon vanilla extract
2 ice cubes

Method

1. Combine chocolate milk, melted chocolate, banana, vanilla extract, and ice cubes in the tall glass. Process in the NutriBullet for 10-12 seconds or until mixture becomes smooth.
2. Transfer mixture in a serving glass.
3. Serve and enjoy!

Dried Fruits Oats and Cinnamon Smoothie

Dried fruits are a great source of fiber, vitamins and antioxidants. They are packed not only with nutrients, but also with flavors because with drying, the fruit's flavor becomes more intense.

Preparation Time: 5 minutes
Total Time: 5 minutes
Yield:1 serving

Ingredients

2 tablespoons raisins
2 tablespoons dried cranberries
2 tablespoons rolled oats
¾ cup skim milk
¼ teaspoon cinnamon, ground

Method

1. Soak the dried fruits and oats in one cup of skim milk for a few hours.
2. Then transfer in the tall glass together with the rest of the ingredients. Process in the NutriBullet for 10-12 seconds or until mixture becomes smooth.
3. Transfer mixture in a serving glass.
4. Serve and enjoy!

Cottage Berry Duo Smoothie

This smoothie has a rich creamy flavor from the cottage cheese and berries. Your kids will be delighted for sure!

Preparation Time: 5 minutes
Total Time: 5 minutes
Yield:1 serving

Ingredients

½ cup frozen strawberries
½ cup cottage cheese
½ cup whole milk
1 teaspoon honey

Method

1. Place strawberries, cottage cheese, milk, and honey in the tall glass. Process in the NutriBullet for 10-12 seconds or until mixture becomes smooth.
2. Pour in a serving glass.
3. Serve and enjoy!

Pineapple Yogurt and Almond Shake

Pineapple is one of the healthiest tropical fruits that you can easily find and when combined with yogurt and almond milk, it yields a delicious and refreshing drink that is beneficial for your kid's tummy.

Preparation Time: 5 minutes
Total Time: 5 minutes
Yield:1 serving

Ingredients

½ cup pineapple chunks
½ cup Greek yogurt
½ cup almond milk
2 ice cubes

Method

1. Combine all the ingredients in your Nutribullet and pulse for 30-40 seconds until well blended.
2. Pour the drink in glasses and serve it immediately.

Cantaloupe and Fresh Mint Smoothie

Refreshing and rehydrating are the initial benefit of this smoothie, along with its high content of vitamins and minerals.

Preparation Time: 5 minutes
Total Time: 5 minutes
Yield:1 serving

Ingredients

¾ cup cantaloupe, diced
½ cup whole milk
¼ cup yogurt
1 mint sprig

Method

1. Mix all the ingredients together in your Nutribullet and process 10-12 seconds or until well blended and smooth.
2. Pour in glasses and serve it as fresh as possible.

Calcium-rich Smoothie Recipe

This delicious recipe is rich in calcium that promotes stronger bones and teeth especially in children.

Preparation Time: 5 minutes
Total Time: 5 minutes
Yield:1 serving

Ingredients

1 handful spinach
3 broccoli florets
1 medium apple, cored and diced
½ cup pineapple chunks
½ cup yogurt
water to max line

Method

1. Place all ingredients in the Nutribullet tall glass.
2. Process for 10-12 seconds or until smooth.
3. Transfer in a serving glass. Enjoy.

Berry Ricotta and Almond Shake

Delicate and healthy, this smoothie tastes like cheesecake. It's thick, creamy and absolutely delicious. Your kids will love it!

Preparation Time: 5 minutes
Total Time: 5 minutes
Yield:1 serving

Ingredients

¼ cup blackberries
¼ cup blueberries
¼ cup ricotta cheese
½ cup whole milk
1 teaspoon honey
2 ice cubes

Method

1. Combine all the ingredients in your Nutribullet and pulse until smooth.
2. Pour the drink in glasses of your choice and serve it right away.

Healthy Blueberry Banana and Almond Smoothie

This blast of blueberry banana smoothie is certainly a kid-friendly recipe.

Preparation Time: 5 minutes
Total Time: 5 minutes
Yield:1 serving

Ingredients

½ cup frozen blueberries
½ medium banana, cut into small pieces
½ cup almond milk
¼ cup Greek yogurt

Method

1. Place all ingredients in the Nutribullet.
2. Process for 10-12 seconds or until smooth.
3. Transfer in a serving glass.
4. Enjoy.

Raspberry and Lemon Smoothie for Kids

This smoothie recipe with raspberries and lemon is rich in vitamin C that helps boost immunity against diseases.

Preparation Time: 5 minutes
Total Time: 5 minutes
Yield:1 serving

Ingredients

½ cup frozen raspberries
2 tsp. lemon juice
½ cup Greek yogurt
½ cup whole milk
1 teaspoon honey

Method

1. Combine all the ingredients in your Nutribullet and process 10-12 seconds or until well blended and smooth.
2. Pour in your choice of glass.
3. Serve immediately.

Blackberry Banana Soy Yogurt Smoothie Recipe

This lactose-free smoothie recipe with blackberries, banana, and soy yogurt makes a yummy and healthy snack for kids!

Preparation Time: 5 minutes
Total Time: 5 minutes
Yield:1 serving

Ingredients

¾ cup frozen blackberries
1 small medium banana, cut into small pieces
2/3 cup soy yogurt, vanilla flavor
water to max line

Method

1. Place blackberries, banana, soy yogurt, and water onto the tall glass. Process in the NutriBullet for 10-12 seconds or until combined well.
2. Pour in a chilled glass. Garnish with few blackberries, if desired.
3. Serve and enjoy!

Berry Peanut Butter and Oat Smoothie

This smoothie is rich in taste and filling and it has a high nutritional content that includes fiber, antioxidants, and protein.

Preparation Time: 5 minutes
Total Time: 5 minutes
Yield:1 serving

Ingredients

½ cup fresh or frozen berries
2 tablespoons peanut butter
2 tablespoons rolled oats
2/3 cupwhole milk

Method

1. Combine all the ingredients in your Nutribullet and pulse until well blended and smooth.
2. Pour in your favorite glass and serve immediately.

Berry Watermelon Blast

There is nothing better than a glass of this juice during hot summer days. It's rehydrating and delicious, perfect for summer when the watermelon is in season.

Preparation Time: 5 minutes
Total Time: 5 minutes
Yield:1 serving

Ingredients

½ cup frozen mixed berries
3/4 cup seedless watermelon, diced
1teaspoon lime juice
1 teaspoon honey
water to max line

Method

1. Place all ingredients in the NutriBullet tall glass.
2. Process for 10-12 seconds or until smooth.
3. Transfer in a serving glass.
4. Enjoy.

Berry and Spinach Smoothie for Kids

Kids don't quite love spinach, but there are ways to hide it efficiently in smoothie, this recipe being one that shows you how. As long as you make sure that the main ingredient has an intense aroma able to mask the flavor of the spinach, any other fruit works.

Preparation Time: 5 minutes

Total Time: 5 minutes
Yield:1 serving

Ingredients

½ cup frozen mixed berries
1 handful spinach
½ medium banana
½ cup yogurt
1 teaspoon maple syrup
water to max line

Method

1. Place all ingredients in the NutriBullet.
2. Process for 10-12 seconds or until smooth.
3. Transfer in a serving glass. Enjoy.

Banana Raspberry Smoothie Recipe

Raspberry smoothie recipes work great with bananas as it changes their consistency into a smooth and creamy drink that even kids will adore. Additionally, the banana has enough natural sweetness, therefore there is no need to add sugar.

Preparation Time: 5 minutes
Total Time: 5 minutes
Yield:1 serving

Ingredients

½ cup frozen raspberries
½ medium banana, cut into small pieces
½ cup Greek yogurt
¼ cup whole milk
2 ice cubes

Method

1. Place raspberries, banana, yogurt, milk, and ice cubes in the NutriBullet.
2. Process for 10-12 seconds or until smooth.
3. Transfer in a serving glass.
4. Enjoy.

Kiwi Banana Berry Smoothie

A combination of three amazing fruits that's best for breakfasts.

Preparation Time: 5 minutes
Total Time: 5 minutes
Yield:1 serving

Ingredients

1 medium kiwi fruit, sliced

½ medium frozen banana, cut into small pieces
½ cup mixed frozen berries
½ cup whole milk

Method

1. Place the kiwi fruit, banana, berries, and milk in in the NutriBullet.
2. Process for 10-12 seconds or until smooth.
3. Transfer in a serving glass. Enjoy.

Banana Apple and Yogurt Smoothie

Thick and creamy, this smoothie is a real delight to your kids. It's so delicious that they can also have it for dessert!

Preparation Time: 5 minutes
Total Time: 5 minutes
Yield:1 serving

Ingredients

1smallfrozen banana, cut into small pieces
1 small apple, cored, and diced
¾ cup yogurt
1 teaspoon chia seeds

Method

1. Place banana, apple, yogurt, and chia seeds in the tall glass.
2. Process in the Nutribullet for 10-12 seconds or until smooth.
3. Transfer in a serving glass. Enjoy.

Creamy Banana and Raspberry Smoothie for Kids

Children surely love bananas and raspberries, but a drink containing them is more than that because it also has yogurt and milk and it is therefore loaded with protein and probiotics too.

Preparation Time: 5 minutes
Total Time: 5 minutes
Yield:1 serving

Ingredients

1small banana, cut into small pieces
½ cup frozen raspberries
½ cup yogurt
water to max line

Method

1. Place the banana, raspberries, yogurt, and water in the NutriBullet.
2. Process for 10-12 seconds or until smooth.
3. Transfer in a serving glass. Enjoy.

Avocado Pineapple and Almond Smoothie Recipe

Avocado is considered one of the healthiest fruits. This particular avocado smoothie recipe with pineapple and almond makes an excellent snack when you want to give your child something very nutritious and filling.

Preparation Time: 5 minutes
Total Time: 5 minutes

Yield:1 serving

Ingredients

1/8 medium avocado, diced
½ cup pineapple chunks
½ cup almond milk
2 ice cubes

Method

1. Place the avocado, pineapple, almond milk, and ice cubes in the tall glass.
2. Process in the Nutribullet for 10-12 seconds or until smooth.
3. Transfer in a serving glass. Enjoy.

Lychee Banana and Soy Smoothie

This healthy smoothie recipe with lychee, banana, and soy will provide your kids with healthy carbs and antioxidants which helps promote stronger body against infection and disease.

Preparation Time: 5 minutes
Total Time: 5 minutes
Yield:1 serving

Ingredients

5 pieces lychees, pitted
1 small banana, sliced
½ cup soy milk
2 ice cubes

Method

1. Combine the lychees, banana, soy milk, and ice cubes in the tall glass. Process in the NutriBullet for 10-12 seconds or until smooth.
2. Pour in a serving glass. Garnish with some lychees, if desired.
3. Serve and enjoy!

Avocado Banana with Honey Smoothie Recipe

This healthy green smoothie recipe is made with avocado, banana and honey. It is loaded with healthy nutrients that will surely give your child an energy boost in the morning before going to school.

Preparation Time: 5 minutes
Total Time: 5 minutes
Yield:1 serving

Ingredients

1/8 medium ripe avocado, peeled, stoned, diced
1 small banana, sliced
1teaspoon lemon juice
1 teaspoon honey
½ cup whole milk
¼ cup crushed ice

Method

1. Place avocado, banana, lemon juice, honey, milk, and crushed icein the tall glass. Process in the NutriBullet for 10-12 seconds or until combined well.
2. Pour in a chilled glass.
3. Serve and enjoy!

Avocado and Raspberry Smoothie for Kids

Avocado is amazing for kids because not only it has a subtle taste, but it is also loaded with nutrients, starting with fibers and ending with the much needed good fats. This smoothie is good for the proper functioning of their brain.

Preparation Time: 5 minutes
Total Time: 5 minutes
Yield:1 serving

Ingredients

1/8 avocado, diced
½ cup frozen raspberries
1 teaspoon honey
½ cup whole milk

Method

1. Place all ingredients in the Nutribullet.
2. Process for 10-12 seconds or until smooth.
3. Transfer in a serving glass. Enjoy.

Minty Mango Yogurt Smoothie

This smoothie recipe with Greek yogurt and mango is so delicious that you would want to make some more!

Preparation Time: 5 minutes
Total Time: 5 minutes
Yield:1 serving

Ingredients

½ cup mango, cubed
½ cup Greek yogurt
½ cup whole milk
1 piece fresh mint sprig

Method

1. Mix the ingredients in your NutriBullet and process until well blended and smooth.
2. Pour it in a serving glass. Garnish with mango and mint sprig, if desired.
3. Serve it right away.

Fruity Yogurt Smoothie

Try this awesome smoothie recipe with mixed fruits and yogurt.

Preparation Time: 5 minutes
Total Time: 5 minutes
Yield:1 serving

Ingredients

½ cup mixed berries
½ medium banana, cut into small pieces
½ medium kiwi fruit
½ cup yogurt

Method

1. Place all ingredients in the NutriBullet.
2. Process for 10-12 seconds or until smooth.
3. Transfer in a serving glass. Enjoy.

Fruity Arugula and Fennel Smoothie

A unique combination of fruits and vegetables in one healthy drink.

Preparation Time: 5 minutes
Total Time: 5 minutes
Yield:1 serving

Ingredients

½ medium banana, cut into small pieces
1/8 medium ripe avocado, diced

1 handful arugula, torn
½ cup fennel bulb, shredded
½ cup yogurt
1 teaspoon honey
water to max line

Method

1. Place banana, avocado, arugula, fennel bulb, yogurt, honey, and water in the tall glass.
2. Process in the Nutribullet for 10-12 seconds or until smooth.
3. Transfer in a serving glass. Enjoy.

Ginger and Orange Smoothie for Kids

Ginger is a wonder spice thanks to its high content of antioxidants and it tastes great too with any citrus fruit. This smoothie is very refreshing, but also highly nutritious.

Preparation Time: 5 minutes
Total Time: 5 minutes
Yield:1 serving

Ingredients

1 medium orange, cut into segments
½ teaspoon ginger, grated
½ cup yogurt
1 teaspoon honey
½ cup crushed ice

Method

1. Combine the orange, ginger, yogurt, honey and crushed ice in your Nutribullet and process for 10-12 seconds or until well blended and smooth.
2. Pour the drink in a glass of your choice.
3. Serve immediately.

Fruit and Vegetable Mix Smoothie

Another wonderful smoothie with fruits and vegetables that contains high amounts of fiber, vitamins, and minerals.

Preparation Time: 5 minutes
Total Time: 5 minutes
Yield:1 serving

Ingredients

1 handful Romaine lettuce, shredded
1/3 medium cucumber, diced
½ cup pineapple chunks
½ medium apple, cored and diced
1 Tbsp. lemon juice
1 tsp. honey
coconutwater to max line

Method

1. Place the lettuce, cucumber, pineapple chunks, apple, lemon juice, honey, and coconut water in the Nutribullet.
2. Process for 10-12 seconds or until smooth.
3. Transfer in a serving glass. Enjoy.

Frozen Mango Yogurt Smoothie

The recipe is simple and the mango is the star but I guess that is precisely what makes it so good – simplicity. However, the nutritional content is high that ranges from fiber to antioxidants and probiotics.

Preparation Time: 5 minutes
Total Time: 5 minutes
Yield:1 serving

Ingredients

2/3 cup frozen mango, diced
½ medium frozen banana, cut into small pieces
½ cup yogurt
¼ cup whole milk

Method

1. Place the mango, banana, yogurt, and milk in the Nutribullet.
2. Process for 10-12 seconds or until smooth.
3. Transfer in a serving glass.
4. Enjoy.

Frozen Berry Smoothie Recipe

This delicious smoothie is made with a mix of frozen berries, yogurt and honey. It makes a perfect breakfast or afternoon snack for the kids.

Preparation Time: 5 minutes
Total Time: 5 minutes
Yield:1 serving

Ingredients

2/3 cup mixed frozen berries
½ medium banana, sliced
½ cup vanilla yogurt
1 teaspoon honey
water to max line

Method

1. Place the mixed berries, banana, yogurt, honey, and water in the Nutribullet.
2. Process for 10-12 seconds or until smooth.
3. Transfer in a serving glass. Enjoy.

All Season Fruit Shake Recipe

This is a nutritious and delicious fruit shake that your kids can enjoy anytime.

Preparation Time: 5 minutes
Total Time: 5 minutes
Yield:1 serving

Ingredients

½ cup papaya, diced
½ cup pineapple chunks
½ cup fresh orange juice
2 ice cubes

Method

1. Combine papaya, pineapple, orange juice, and ice cubes in the Nutribullet.
2. Process for 10-12 seconds or until smooth.
3. Transfer in a serving glass. Enjoy.

Cucumber Watermelon and Yogurt Smoothie

This smoothie recipe with cucumber, watermelon, lime, and yogurt will not only keep your kids hydrated but refreshed as well. Very nice to have especially when the weather is hot.

Preparation Time: 5 minutes
Total Time: 5 minutes
Yield:1 serving

Ingredients

1 cup seedless watermelon, cubed
1/3 medium cucumber, deseeded, diced
½ cup Greek yogurt, vanilla
1 teaspoon lime

Method

1. Place watermelon, cucumber, Greek yogurt, and lime into the tall glass. Process in the NutriBullet for 10-12 seconds or until becomes smooth.
2. Pour in a chilled serving glass. Garnish with a slice of watermelon or cucumber, if desired.
3. Serve and enjoy!

Cucumber Celery and Apple Smoothie for Kids

Don't underestimate cucumber and celery. Both have high content of water and minerals and that makes this recipe an amazing summer drink.

Preparation Time: 5 minutes
Total Time: 5 minutes
Yield:1 serving

Ingredients

½ medium cucumber, sliced
1 medium green apple, cored and diced
1 small celery stalk diced
2 teaspoons lime juice
1 teaspoon honey
2 ice cubes
water to max line

Method

1. Combine the cucumber, apple,celery, lime juice, honey, and water in your Nutribullet and process until well blended and smooth.
2. Pour in a glass of your choice and serve it right away.

Coconut and Strawberry Smoothie for Kids

Delicate and nutritious, this smoothie is a good source of antioxidants and fiber, but also good fats. It's delicious and your child will have no problem enjoying it.

Preparation Time: 5 minutes
Total Time: 5 minutes
Yield:1 serving

Ingredients

½ cup strawberries, halved
½ medium banana, cut into small pieces
2tablespoons coconut milk
½ cup coconut water
1 teaspoon honey

Method

1. Combine the strawberries, banana, coconut milk, coconut water, and honey in your Nutribullet.
2. Process for 10-12 seconds or until the drink is well blended and smooth.
3. Pour the smoothie in a glass of your choice and serve right away.

Cocoa and Banana Smoothie for Kids

Pure, good quality cocoa powder or chocolate is a great source of antioxidants, but it also has a rather bitter taste, therefore it works better combined with sweet fruits, banana being one of the best options.

Preparation Time: 5 minutes
Total Time: 5 minutes

Yield:1 serving

Ingredients

1 medium banana, cut into small pieces
1 tablespoon cocoa powder+ 2 tablespoons hot water
2/3 cup almond milk
1 teaspoon honey
2 ice cubes

Method

1. Combine the banana, cocoa powder, almond milk, honey, and ice cubes in your Nutribullet.
2. Process for 10-12 seconds or until smoothie is smooth.
3. Pour in a glass of your choice and serve immediately.

Citrus Smoothie for Kids

Tangy, loaded with antioxidants and fiber, this smoothie is a real delight for children.

Preparation Time: 5 minutes
Total Time: 5 minutes
Yield:1 serving

Ingredients

½ medium orange, cut into segments
½ medium grapefruit, cut into segments

½ cup yogurt
1 teaspoon honey
2 ice cubes

Method

1. Combine all the ingredients in your Nutribullet and process 10-12 seconds or until well blended and smooth.
2. Pour it in a serving glass.
3. Serve immediately.

Chocolate Banana Milkshake Recipe

Chocolate and bananas is a delicious combination loved by most people and it makes a great choice for breakfast just because it's nutritious and very filling.

Preparation Time: 5 minutes
Total Time: 5 minutes
Yield:1 serving

Ingredients

1 large banana
2 tablespoons dark chocolate, melted
½ cup whole milk
¼ cup plain yogurt

Method

1. Place the banana, milk, yogurt, and dark chocolate in the tall glass.
2. Process in theNutribullet until smooth and creamy.
3. Pour in a serving glass.
4. Serve immediately.

Carrot and Banana Smoothie for Kids

Both carrot and banana are rather sweet so you can skip adding any other sweetener to this drink. It's a rich and creamy smoothie, an amazing drink any time of the day.

Preparation Time: 5 minutes
Total Time: 5 minutes
Yield:1 serving

Ingredients

½ medium carrot, diced
½ medium banana, cut into small pieces
½ cup whole milk
½ cup vanilla yogurt
2 ice cubes

Method

1. Combine carrot, banana, milk, yogurt, and ice cubes in the Nutribullet.
2. Process for 10-12 seconds or until smooth.
3. Transfer in a serving glass. Enjoy.

Kiwi Banana and Kale Smoothie for Kids

Just like spinach, kale is not the first choice of kids when it comes to veggies, but it is a healthy addition to your child's diet so it's worth the effort of introducing it to the child. This particular smoothie combines the sweetness of kiwi and banana with kale, creating a drink that is both delicious and nutritious.

Preparation Time: 5 minutes
Total Time: 5 minutes
Yield:1 serving

Ingredients

1 medium kiwi, peeled and diced
½ medium banana, cut into small pieces
1 handful kale, torn
½ cup yogurt
1 teaspoon honey
water to max line

Method

1. Combinekiwi, banana, kale, yogurt, honey, and water in your Nutribullet. Process 10-12 seconds or until well blended
2. Pour in a chilled serving glass.
3. Serve immediately.

Pumpkin Smoothie for Children

If your child likes pumpkin, this smoothie will be a real delight. It's rich and absolutely delicious, loaded with nutrients and autumn flavors.

Preparation Time: 5 minutes
Total Time: 5 minutes
Yield:1 serving

Ingredients

½ cup pumpkin puree
½ medium banana, cut into small pieces
¼ cup whole milk
¼ cup crushed ice

Method

1. Combine the pumpkin puree, banana, milk, and ice in your Nutribullet and process 10-12 seconds or until well blended and smooth.
2. Pour the drink in glass of your choice and serve right away.

Apple Pie Smoothie for Kids

Apple may be a common fruit, but it also one of the healthiest. If your kids don't like eating it raw, how about a smoothie that contains it and tastes like apple pie?!

Preparation Time: 5 minutes
Total Time: 5 minutes
Yield:1 serving

Ingredients

1 medium apple, cored and cut into small pieces
½ cup yogurt
¼ cup whole milk
dash of cinnamon, ground

Method

1. Combine the apple, yogurt, milk, and cinnamon in your Nutribullet and process 10-12 seconds or until well blended and smooth.
2. Pour in a serving glass.
3. Serve right away because it tends to change color in time.

Fruity Yogurt and Oat Smoothie for Kids

Yogurt is a wonder food for children in need of a stronger immune system. Thanks to its high content of probiotics, yogurt helps with digestion and we all know that a good digestive system means a better immunity.

Preparation Time: 5 minutes
Total Time: 5 minutes
Yield:1 serving

Ingredients

½ cup Greek yogurt
1 medium apple, cored and diced
4 pieces strawberries, halved
1 tablespoon rolled oats

Method

1. Combine yogurt, apple, strawberries, and oats in your Nutribullet and process for 10-12 seconds or until well blended.
2. Pour the smoothie in a serving glass
3. Serve right away.

Made in the USA
Middletown, DE
24 January 2022

59538882R00116